Exam Practice

TYPEWRITING SKILLS STAGE I

RSA

HEINEMANN EDUCATIONAL

in association with RSA Examinations Board

Heinemann Educational,
a division of Heinemann Educational Books Ltd,
Halley Court, Jordan Hill, Oxford OX2 8EJ

OXFORD LONDON EDINBURGH
MELBOURNE SYDNEY AUCKLAND
IBADAN NAIROBI GABORONE HARARE
KINGSTON PORTSMOUTH NH (USA)
SINGAPORE MADRID

First published 1989
Reprinted 1989, 1990

British Library Cataloguing in Publication Data
Typewriting Skills Stage I.
1. Typing – Manuals
I. Title II. Series
652.3

ISBN 0-435-45150-2

Produced by DMD, Oxford
Printed by Thomson Litho Ltd, Scotland

Contents

Introduction

This book provides practice in the types of task included in RSA Stage I Typewriting Skills examinations and the keying-in tasks in Stage I Word Processing examinations. The material has been specially compiled by a group of Chief Examiners currently involved in these examinations.

RSA Examinations Board records its thanks to Margaret Rees-Boughton, Consultant to RSA for Office Subjects, for her work in the origination of the book and in editing it, and to the following Chief Examiners:

Phillip Arnold
Lesley Dakin
Tessa Greig
Susan North
and
Beryl Whittick

Checking

Remember: you cannot regard your work as satisfactory until you have checked the text you have typed and corrected any keyboarding errors.

Worked examples are provided at the back of the book, so that you can also check if you have interpreted correctly all of the instructions and the handwriting in each task.

NB: In exams, you must always leave a left margin (at least half-inch). It may not always have been possible to show this in the printed worked examples.

Stationery

The RSA exam letterhead, memo and general forms suitable for use with the exercises in this book are available from bookshops. If you should experience any difficulty, then contact the publishers.

RSA Exam Practice

This book is one of a series in which RSA provides practice material based on tasks in RSA exams in Typewriting Skills and Word Processing.

1 Letters and memos

Notes to candidates

In the exam, the letter and memo may be on the same subject, and they may be drafted as from the same person.

The draft will include an instruction to take a carbon copy of one of these documents, and to type an envelope.

It is necessary to produce the carbon copy in order to pass the exam. In addition to correcting the other documents you need to make any necessary corrections to your own typing in the carbon copy so that it is an accurate copy. The carbon copy should be typed on the yellow flimsy paper provided in the exam.

If the envelope is requested for a document with a special mark, eg URGENT, this special mark must also be typed on the envelope. It is also necessary to copy the use of capitals in the exam draft, eg for the postal town.

In the exam you will be provided with enough stationery to make a second attempt at each task, if you need to do so. However, there will be only one envelope in the stationery pack, so you must try to complete the typing of this in one attempt. If you totally spoil the envelope, however, you should re-type the proper details on a piece of plain paper.

Aim to type, check and correct a letter, memo, envelope and carbon copy within 45 minutes.

00.45

Task 1.1 – letter

Ref: BD/433

Envelope, and carbon copy on yellow paper with this letter, please

Mrs Janet Moores
Moores & Evans plc
LOWER CLIFTON
Worcs
WR12 6EQ

Dear Mrs Moores

PRAXITELES OPERA GROUP

two sets of complimentary opera
Your ⁄ tickets are enclosed. // The works ~~which we are putting on this year~~ being performed are MEDEA by Cherubini and ALBERT HERRING by Britten. I bel. that these will be the first performances of both ~~works~~ operas in this region.

Those taking the major roles are:

Mary Golding as Medea,
Norman Reid as Jason,
Mike Bishop as Albert,
Daphne Lane as Lady Billows.

Inset 5 spaces from left margin

require any more tickets please contact
If you shd. ~~need to book further seats telephone~~ the sec. of the opera group. Seat prices are £7.50 and £5.00. There is a 10% discount for party bookings of 15 or more. As a sponsor of the opera group you will rec. free programmes. Please collect these from the box office on arrival.

I am sure that you and your guests will enjoy these very different works. The one is high tragedy and the other is a comedy. I very much look forward to meeting you and your guests.

Yrs. sinc.
Praxiteles Group

Barbara Davis
Group Secretary

From Jane Fellows　　　　Ref JF/POG

To Barbara Davis　　　　(Memo)

URGENT

Opera Plot Outlines

Below are plot outlines of the two works being performed this year.

I think these should def. be added to the cast lists. The co. is giving these to all employees coming next Tues. and Thurs. to the dress rehearsals.

"Medea is a Greek sorceress. Her husband Jason ~~abandons her for another woman whose name is Glauce~~ leaves her and she kills his children and new wife in revenge.

"Albert Herring is crowned King of the May. He spends his prize money on (debauchery and drinking) that night. This helps free him from his nagging mother."

I would be very grateful if this could be done today as the cast lists are ~~since all the other information is~~ ready for printing.

Programmes for both operas have now been printed and copies for sponsors will be sent up to you. These are to be left at the box office.

Ref SA/LC/88

TYPIST: Carbon Copy on yellow flimsy and Envelope please.

Miss Louise Cooke
21 Calverton Cres.
Brampton Bierlow
ROTHERHAM
South Yorkshire S62 3QP

Dr. Miss Cooke

Service Agreement – Vauxhall Nova

Congratulations on choosing to buy one of our cars. You will get many hours of ~~pleasant and enjoyable~~ pleasure and safe motoring from this car. // The main ingredient for safe motoring ~~lies with~~ is ~~normal~~ regular servicing. The makers recom. a service every 12 months or 9,000 miles. Michael Oliver, our senior salesman, should already have told you about these limits at the time of the sale. He should also have given you a catalogue. The cat. shows the benefits of our Fixed Price Service programme.

The mfrs. have approved service limits for this model. To benefit from your breakdown insurance you must keep within these limits. There is an allowable leeway (of 700 miles or 14 days) either side of the agreed mileage and time periods.

TYPIST: INSET 10 Spaces

The policy may be CANCELLED if these limits are not met.

In closing, it is the sole aim of our team to ensure that this deal is only the start of a long association. I hope that ~~resulting from the quality of our after sales service~~ you will consider us for your future car purchases.

Yrs. sincerely

James Powers
General Sales Manager

Task 1.4 – memo

From James Powers (MEMO) Ref SA/LC/88
General Sales Manager

To John Porter
Service Department

URGENT

Service Agreement - Vauxhall Nova

You wl. see from the attached letter ~~dated to Mr~~ that Miss Louise Cooke has taken out our fully extended mechanical breakdown insurance in ~~respect~~ of her Vauxhall Nova car. This shd. take effect from the (day and time) of purchase.

(✓) However, she wishes to have her car ~~checked~~ ~~serviced~~ at her local garage instead of at our workshop.)

(I have refd. this to Mr Key, our Managing Director, for his review. I feel that in order to gntee. the insurance cover Miss Cooke should have her car checked with us. I will let you know the outcome of my letter to Mr Key.

Task 1.5 – memo

From Tony Stone Ref TS/BVR (MEMO)
To Angela Robson

FRANKFURT CAR STUDY

You will by now have recd. a copy of the letter which we are about to send out to all ~~the participants~~ those taking part in the above project who live in the south-east region. ~~Please go ahead now with the final travel details.~~ The tickets and itinerary details shd. be sent out early next week.

I wd. remind you that you must have a cheque for £25 ready for each passenger on arrival at Gatwick.)

(These cheques are to pay for travelling expenses and parking fees. On the last trip ~~there were problems because~~ these cheques were not to hand when we arrived back at the home airport. This time they (all/must) be ready before the passengers leave the airport for their homes. Make sure that you thank each one individually for

(✓) their help in this ~~very~~ important project.

Task 1.6 – letter

Take a carbon copy on yellow paper & type an envelope

Our ref TS/BVR

PERSONAL

Mrs Stella Rowe
The Warden
6 Saxton Court
EAST GRINSTEAD
Sussex RH29 3BY

Dear Mrs Rowe

FRANKFURT CAR STUDY

Praxi Research is a British market research agency. It carries out surveys for gov. departments and leading bus. concerns. ~~In this instance~~ At present we are working on a study in Frankfurt.

Thank you for helping us w. this new project. Our purpose is to get the opinions of owners about certain new cars. We hope that you will treat this as an opp. to pass on your views to the mfrs. about their products.

The ~~study~~ takes the form of a motor show at wh. you will be asked to fill in a form giving your views on the new cars. [No one will try to sell you anything, either now or later, as a result of this.

INSET 6 SPACES

You will leave Gatwick Airport at 8.00 am.
The flight will take about two hours.
The return flight will leave at 2.30 pm.

We feel sure that you will have an interesting and rewarding day. Enclosed are some further details.

Yours scly.
TONY STONE

FIELD DIRECTOR

Task 1.7 – letter

Ref CLTY/234

TYPIST: Carbon copy on yellow flimsy, and Env please

URGENT

Miss Rita Jackson
21 Lavender Close
LEAMINGTON SPA
Warwickshire
CV31 9EA

Dr. Miss Jackson

Post of Typist/Clerk - Purchasing Department

I ack. rec. of your letter of ~~22 July applying~~ application dated yesterday for the above post. I have had many suitable replies. I would like to start interviewing during the next week. I have arranged the following appt. ~~time~~ for you:

Typist: INSET 6 SPACES TUESDAY of next week at 10.30 am.

If either the date or the time is awkward would you please contact my secretary, Miss Jane Landers, ~~on extension 376~~ as soon as possible. She will then allot a new time wh. will suit you and still fit in with my time schedule. // I would be grateful if you wd. bring along your certificates. You will be required to take a short typing test. The test may be taken on a manual or electronic machine.

After the first talk and test you may be asked to attend our medical office to undergo a full medical. In order to reduce the time involved for this medical would you please complete the enclosed form and bring it with you.

Yours sincerely

David Harrison
PERSONNEL MANAGER

Task 1.8 – memo

From David Harrison
Personnel

MEMO

Ref CLTY/234

To Dr Janet Munro
Medical

Post of Clerk Typist – Purchasing Department

I have arranged to see all the suitable applicants for the above post during next week. I bel. that the best time for you to conduct the medicals is after lunch.

However, I am not able to see everyone in the afternoon. Most of the interviews are ~~planned~~ ~~scheduled~~ for 10.30 am. (2.30 pm ~~but three~~ are for)

I am sending a medical form to each applicant w.a request to complete the form & ~~to~~ bring it to the interview. As each person arrives, I wl. get my sec. ~~Miss Sanders~~ to let you have the form straight away. You wl. then have enough time to study it.

Task 1.9 – memo

FROM Publicity Manager

Ref TJ/CD

MEMO

TO Accounts

EXPENSE ACCOUNTS

I enclose a list of my exps. incurred during my bus. trip to Germany. I have obtained ~~managed to obtain~~ recs. for the majority of my expenses. I have not claimed ~~any expenses~~ for travelling from and to the airport because a chauffeur was provided.

As you can see from the list, the amount is considerable and I would appreciate immediate refund of this money. Perhaps in future I cd. be allowed to have an advance in respect of expenses to be incurred. I look forward to hearing your views on this request.

Task 1.10 – letter

Ref GM/GLD

URGENT

TYPIST: Carbon copy on yellow flimsy. Env please.

Mr J Brough
12 Midway Close
LEICESTER
LE1 7RJ

Dear Sir

I am writing to confirm the arrangements for the meeting w. the clients. This will take place at their offices on ~~Monday 7 June~~ Friday 28 May at 10.15 am. I have asked the clients to let me know in wh. room the meeting is to be held. I wl. contact you again when this data is to hand.

I understand that the clients would like to have a hint of your findings. They would like the opp. of making comments prior to the final preparation of your report.

The clients are particularly keen to have this meeting because ~~as I think you know~~ they differ with certain of Mr Hooley's comments about the roofs. We did, of course, briefly discuss this on the phone a little while ago.// A meeting has been arranged for 11 June. If possible, the Council would like your report to be available for discussion. The Council has requested 3 dozen copies of your report.

with the members of the Council

TYPIST: INSET 5 Spaces

Will it be possible to produce this number?
Will your report include reference to photographs?

If so, do you think it would be ~~preferable~~ better to have 3 or 4 sep. sets of photographs, rather than to produce 3 dozen sets? I wd. be grateful for your comments in this respect.

I look forward to hearing from you.

Yours faithfully

Gerald Mortison

Task 1.11 – letter

Ref. P3/PH/VK

(Carbon copy on yellow flimsy. Env. please.)

PERSONAL

Dr & Mrs Robert Binns
Peppercorn Cottage
Alrewas Rd.
NOTTINGHAM
NG2 4VX

Dear Dr & Mrs Binns

I am writing to offer you, as valued customers, the opportunity to take out a Praxiloan of up to £3,000 to spend on almost anything you like.

A Praxiloan means that you can put ~~many of~~ your ideas into action **NOW**. You can spread the loan ~~from~~ (five) to (one) years. (over any period to suit you)

If you borrow ~~£5,000 over two years~~ £3,000 over one year yr. repayments will be around £275 per month. For the ~~same~~ amount over five yrs. you will pay £75 monthly. ~~Just let me know beforehand~~.

For peace of mind your repayments can be ~~covered~~ protected with our own safeguard scheme for only a modest extra charge. This scheme ensures that in the events of illness, accident or even unemployment your repayments will be made for you.

(Typist: Inset 12 spaces) APPLY for your Praxiloan NOW!

To arrange your loan, complete and return the enclosed application form as soon as possible. [If you let us know when you need the money we will make the funds immed. ready for your use.

Yours sincerely

Peter Howard
Loans Manager

Task 1.12 – memo

FROM Peter Howard

Memo

Ref PH/VK

To Gail Wright
Personal Loans Department

Advertising Campaign

I have instructed that all members on our books are sent the necy. papers inviting them to apply for a loan. I believe that many requests will come from people wishing to book a holiday abroad. We have suff. funds at the ~~present time~~ moment to finance 25 such loans.

All applications from students for temp. loans shd. be considered with care. You must judge each case on its own merit.

However, I must ask you to ensure that students are capable of making regular payments. I suggest you make Charlotte Worthing resp. for vetting all requests.

Members of staff do not qualify to apply for the Praxiloan on offer. Alternative arrangements are being made for staff and wl. be disclosed shortly.

Task 1.13 – memo

From Personnel Manager
To All members of staff
Ref KL/EN

MEMO

CUTTING COMMUTING COSTS

I bel. that the majority of our staff use public transport to travel to and from work. They know that buying an annual season ticket could save them money. I ack. that the initial cost can be formidable. (of making such a saving)
~~They probably buy weekly season tickets~~

I have discussed this with other senior members of staff. We have agreed to recom. that the company shd. consider a scheme whereby loans can be made available. Loans wd. be at a fixed interest rate. This would be lower than the current rate.

The table enclosed gives examples. I emphasise that the amount payable would not change if ~~rates of interest~~ interest rates ~~go~~ went up or down.

This concession would not apply to temporary staff.

The sum representing your loan plus the interest would be added together and then divided by 12. The answer gives ~~the details of~~ your final monthly repayments.

To qualify, you need to be 18 yrs. of age or over.

If you are interested, please let me know by the end of the week.

Task 1.14 – letter

Carbon copy on yellow paper and an envelope please

Our ref ST/ACM

PRIVATE

Miss Veronica Baxter

6 Woburn Hill

CIRENCESTER

Glos

GL7 1SKY

Dear Miss Baxter

ACCOUNT NUMBER B42976V

✓ Many of our cardholders have found that the ~~credit~~ limits on their cards are now too low for their needs. They have written to ask for an increase.

For this reason we have reviewed our limits for all our cardholders. // To try to ensure that ~~these meet~~ we meet our customers' needs, we have chosen certain a/cs. where a higher limit wd. appear to be appropriate.

INSET 12 SPACES [As a result your own limit has been increased to £950. This takes immed. effect. We do hope that you will find this extra credit helpful.

I am sure you agree that using your Praxicard is a safer method of paying for goods than carrying cash or cheques in your wallet or handbag.

Yrs. scly.

Stephen Turner

PRAXICARD CHIEF EXECUTIVE

Task 1.15 – letter

(Take a carbon copy on yellow paper.)

(Type an envelope)

Our ref C/92805

Mr Leonard Coleman
18 Richmond Avenue
BRISTOL
BS28 4BW

Dear Mr Coleman

ORDER C/92805

Thank you for yr. recent order which was recd. today. I am very sorry to have to write to tell you that I have to delay this order.

I have refd. to the electoral register. I bel. that it ~~seems to be possible~~ may be that an error has been made in the detail of your address. I am, of course, concerned in case such an error shd. result in the goods being sent to the wrong address. // Will you please confirm that the [statements] [following] are correct.

INSET 5 SPACES

The above address is correct.

You have lived there at least a year. ~~If you have not lived there~~

(✓) If either of these statements is incorrect, please let me know. If you have moved recently, please give me ~~full~~ details of your previous address.

I apologise most sincerely for any incon. caused to you. I hope you appreciate that it is necessary that we take precautions to ensure that such a valuable order does not go astray.

A stamped addressed envelope is enclosed.

Yours sincerely
LILIAN BONNER

Praxi Consumer Services Manager

Task 1.16 – memo

From Despatch Department
To Customer Services
Ref C/92805

MEMO

URGENT

I set out below details of a new customer.

Mr Leonard Coleman
18 Richmond Avenue
BRISTOL
BS28 4BW

It is necy. for a check to be made on this address. It does not appear on the electoral register.

This is in a new housing area. Only numbers 2 to 16 are listed. It may be th. it was once a showhome wh. has now been sold.

If the address proves to be genuine, we can assume that Mr Coleman moved ~~to the new address~~ less than a yr. ago. If so, we will need details of his previous address.

You will no doubt remember there have been occasions when goods have been ordered and sent to an empty house.

The keys had been obtained from the ~~estate agency~~ selling agents.
We are therefore checking on all orders over the value of £100.

Task 1.17 – memo

MEMO

From James Foster, Praxi Investment Department Manager
To Branch Managers
JF/DR

J PLUS BONDS

You will by now have had details of the new J PLUS BONDS. I am hoping th. most of these will be taken up by ~~clients who hold our current~~ members of Praxi Plus Fund.

I have been in touch with all holders of shares in this fund. ~~Some have been advised~~ All such clients should by now have had a leaflet on J Plus. I am hoping that this will lead to a considerable number of enquiries over the next few months. A supply of the leaflets is being sent to you under sep. cover today.

I would remind you ~~that we are keen~~ to take every opportunity to promote these bonds. If these are not suitable for the ~~purpose~~, offer the alternative of our current ~~monthly~~ income bonds.

Task 1.18 – letter

JF/DR

Carbon copy on yellow paper please. Type an envelope

CONFIDENTIAL

Mrs Karen Howard
13 Royston Street
STOCKPORT
Cheshire   SK3 19CZ

Dear Mrs Howard

PRAXI PLUS FUND

The Praxi Plus Fund account wh. you opened with us just under 5 yrs. ago will mature at the end of next month. My main purpose in writing to you today is to thank you for yr. support during that time. I would like also to tell you what will happen when the a/c. matures.

You do not have to take any immed. action. All you have to do is call at yr. local office. This visit shd. take place before the end of next month. The branch manager (or any member of the staff) will be pleased to help you.

~~If you have already given instructions~~ A leaflet telling you about our newest fund is enclosed. The rate is high.

(Inset 5 spaces) Included is a gntee. of the high differential for the full term of 24 months.

Our local staff will be pleased to discuss details with you. It is not necy. for you to make an appointment. Once again, thank you for your support which I do hope will continue.

Yours sincerely
JAMES FOSTER

Praxi Investment Department Manager

2 Draft notices for display

Notes to candidates

In this type of task you will be instructed to use different styles of capitals, to leave some space clear, and to fill gaps in words which are repeated in the draft.

Make sure you follow all instructions accurately.

Aim to type, check and correct display tasks within 15 minutes. 00.15

Task 2.1

Praxiteles Opera Group (Use A4 plain paper)

SUMMER SEASON ← (Spaced Capitals)

This yr. this opera group is mounting two works. These are "Medea" by Cherubini and "Albert Herring" by Benjamin Britten.

(Leave at least 50 mm (2") here for photographs)

Seat prices are £7.50 and £5.00. There is a 10% reduction for parties (15 or more) and a 50% reduction for children under 13.

Performances are in the Great Hall at Praxiteles House. Praxiteles O—— G—— is an amateur co. with very high standards. It has been favourably compared with the major opera companies.

The last performance of each work is for charity and all proceeds will go to children in need. (caps)

Task 2.2

(A4 plain paper please)

Praxiteles Wildlife Park

OFFERS ← (Typist: spaced capitals please)

25% off normal admission charges during the winter season, October–March.

Lots to see and do! ← (Typist: this line in capitals please)

(Typist: leave at least 100 mm (4") here for an illustration)

Spend a day at Praxiteles W___ P___. Visit the reptile house and aquarium. Take a look at the tigers, lions, pumas, bears, elephants, monkeys, penguins, deer and birds. Don't miss the sea-lion show (every day at 1400 hours). Relax in the tropical gardens. Enjoy a meal in our restaurant and try our tea rooms.

Take this opp. to have a really super day out.

Praxiteles Wildlife Park
Hudson Rd.
SPARKWELL
Plymouth

Telephone: (0653) 40126

Opening hours: 1000-1800 hours daily.

Task 2.3

(plain A4 paper please)

Staff Notice

PRAXITELES SOCIAL CLUB ← (Typist: spaced capitals please)

Sponsored Bed Push ← (Typist: capitals please)

The sponsored bed push held last month raised a grand total of £1001.92 – almost 75% up on last year's total.

Congratulations to all who took part!

Fancy dress prizes were awarded to:

1st Caroline Hold
2nd Peter Edwards.

It has been agreed that 25% of the proceeds shd. be donated to a local charity. As a result, the Committee would welcome suggestions for a worthwhile local charity to receive a donation of £250.00. Please pass on your ideas to the Club Sec., Christine Gill.

↑
(Typist: leave at least 50 mm (2") here)
↓

David Shanks – Chairman
Praxiteles S____ C__

Task 2.4

A4 plain paper please

Spaced capitals

PRAXI PROMOTIONS PRESENT

David and Fred in Concert

Leave at least 38 mm (1½") here

CAPS

The famous rock duo, David and Fred, will be in town shortly for a series of concerts sponsored by Praxi Records Limited.

They will be signing copies of their album, "David and Fred in Concert", at Praxi House on Fri. of next week from 9.30 am – 11.30 am and 2.30 pm – 4.30 pm. You may also rec. signed copies by sending an order with £7.50 for the black disc or £12.50 for the compact disc. Prices include postage.

Address your orders to:

Praxi R______ L______
Praxi House
Adam Street
LONDON
WC2N 6EZ

Typist: use A4 plain white paper please

PRAXITELES FOTO STUDIO ← Typist: capitals but not spaced

proudly announces the opening of its new branch

at

101 St Mary's Rd.
HULL
HU1 2NP

Allow Praxiteles F— S— to help you capture those special moments on film forever:

weddings
baby portraits
anniversaries.

SPECIAL OFFER ← Typist: spaced capitals please

Portrait Sitting

Sitting fee £25

Typist: leave at least 75 mm (3") here for a photograph

Order from mounted slides, colour prints in a variety of sizes, complete with presentation folders and receive absolutely free, one large print, 250 mm x 175 mm.

Why not ring us to make an appt. now? Our phone number is (0482) 718901. We are open Monday–Saturday, 10.00 am–4.00 pm. We are pleased to offer free help and advice.

Task 2.6

Typist: use A4 plain white paper please

leave a top margin of at least 50 mm (2")

Praxiteles Textiles plc

VACANCY ← Typist: spaced capitals please

Secretary to Sales Director ← Typist: capitals please

Salary: £10,000 per annum

Age Range: Over 30

Praxiteles T—— p— is a fast growing company. The Sales Director runs a busy sales office and requires a hard working aide to help him with a heavy work load.

Applicants must have good typing and shorthand skills. A tactful manner and the ability to work under pressure wl. be essential.

The post offers benefits to the value of approx. £3,000 per annum: private health care, share bonus and pension.

Apply in writing to:

Mrs Anita Chan
Box 25
LEEDS
LS2 4NX

(Typist: use plain A4 paper)

PRAXITELES SUN TOURS ← (spaced capitals please)

Hotel Dominque, Neja, Costa del Sol

NOTICE TO CLIENTS

Hello, my name is Sharon.

↑

(Typist: leave at least 75 mm (3") here please for a photograph)

↓

I am your Praxiteles S_ T__ representative here in the Hotel Dominque.

I am available each day except Suns. (my day off), at my desk in the hotel foyer, between the hours of 9.30-11.45 am. I also hold a happy hour at the poolside bar at midday, Mondays-Saturdays, for all new arrivals.

In my absence please find 2 ref. folders and 4 tourist booklets on my desk, which I hope you will find of use.

Regards

Sharon ← (Typist: capitals please)

3 Drafts including tables

Notes to candidates

This type of task tests your ability to present material in columns as well as continuous text.

You will also need to be careful how you allocate space around the columns and other wording so as to fit the work on to A5 paper.
NB: You are not required to rule tables in RSA Stage I exams.

Aim to type, check and correct this type of task within 25 minutes. 00.25

Task 3.1

(Typist: use A5 paper with the shorter edge at the top)

PRAXI FENCING SUPPLIERS

Manufacturers of fencing panels and concrete fencing and garden products.

Save money! Buy direct, with immediate free delivery!

Sample prices given below; other sizes readily available.

Description	Size (feet)	Price
		£
Pine rustic	6 x 6	7.65
Pine rustic	6 x 4	6.80
Closeboard	6 x 6	14.00
Closeboard	6 x 4	19.75
Re-inforced concrete posts	9	5.25
Re-inforced concrete posts	7	4.10
Wooden posts	6	2.50
Wooden posts	8	2.95
Re-inforced concrete gravel boards	6 x 12	3.85
Re-inforced concrete gravel boards	6 x 6	2.80
Patio paving slabs, natural	2 x 2	1.65
Patio paving slabs, coloured	2 x 2	1.70

Task 3.2

Use A5 paper with the longer edge at the top.

DO YOU KNOW YOUR ONIONS?

Onions can be sliced, chopped or grated, eaten raw, fried, roasted or pickled. They vary in texture, flavour and strength, and in shape, type and size.

Nutritionally, onions are excellent. Raw globe onions contain 23 calories per 100 g – though fried ones contain 345 calories per 100 g.

Type	Taste	Time to Buy
Globe	Very pungent and strong	November to February
Spanish	Mild, sweet and crisp	July to April
Silverskins ...	Pungent and strong	September
Italian ...	Mild and sweet	April to May
White ...	Mild and sweet	September to August
Shallots ..	Mellow, sweet and delicate	August to October
Spring onions	Mild and delicate	July to August

Task 3.3

Type on A5 paper with the shorter edge at the top.

FREE FITTING OF ALL OUR TYRES

PRAXITELES TYRE REPLACEMENT

New tyres are adequately speed rated, meeting every European specification; ~~re~~moulds are subjected to rigorous tests, while part-worn tyres are ideally suitable for the spare wheel.

	Size	Price
Firestone	155 x 12	£15.95
Firestone	175 x 13	£19.50
Firestone	185 x 14	£24.95
Goodyear	145 x 10	£14.75
Goodyear	165 x 13	£22.00
Goodyear	155 x 13	£20.95
Dunlop	145 x 10	£14.70
Dunlop	155 x 13	£20.00
Dunlop	165 x 13	£22.00
Remould	185 x 14	£17.50
Part-worn	175 x 14	£10.90
Part-worn	185 x 14	£11.90

Telephone 01 930 5115

PRAXITELES TYRE REPLACEMENT
Adam Street
London
WC2N 6EZ

Task 3.4

Type on A5 paper with the longer edge at the top.

PRAXITELES GROUP - CATERING SERVICE

As requested at the last Group board meeting, the accountant has now prepared a summary of cash forecast for the first 3 months of the new trading year. The figures suggest that earlier concern is borne out and steps must be taken to improve matters. The figures will be discussed in detail next week.

	January	February	March
	£,000	£,000	£,000
Total estimated payments - - - -	9,000	8,000	14,000
Total estimated receipts - - - -	8,500	11,400	9,800
Bank balance at start month - - -	1,000	500	3,900
Excess of receipts over payments (net inflow) - - - - - -		3,400	
Excess of payments over receipts (net outflow) - - - - -	500		4,200
Bank balance at end month - -	500	3,900	300 (overdrawn)

Task 3.5

Typist: please use A5 paper with the shorter edge at the top.

PRAXIGLASS GARDEN POOLS

Bring your garden alive with one of our garden pools. We have developed a new process to create larger, stronger glassfibre pools specially designed to suit every shape and size of garden. Simple to install and guaranteed for 12 years, our pools add charm and magic to your garden.

	Depth	Gallons
Circular	46 cm	100
Square	30 cm	60
Hourglass	51 cm	65
Three-cornered	51 cm	65
Irregular	51 cm	110
Crescent	30 cm	36
Elongated	51 cm	270
Small circular	30 cm	25

To help you decide which pool suits your garden, we have prepared a leaflet illustrating our complete range, including scale drawings for size comparison. Ask for a copy at your nearest garden centre.

Task 3.6

Please use A5 paper with the longer edge at the top.

PRAXITELES GROUP ANNIVERSARY CONFERENCE

Time	Programme	Venue
1000	"50 years in the market place" . . . An illustrated talk by the Sales Director	Sussex Room
1030	"Selling in the Nineties" . . . . . . Introduced by John Harper	Sussex Room
1045	Coffee - - - - - - -	Lounge
1115	Workshops - - - - - - Delegates will be allocated to one of 3 groups	Sussex Room Kent Room Surrey Room
1215	Report back to main meeting - - . Followed by question and answer session	Sussex Room
1300	Lunch - - - - - -	Restaurant
1530	"Looking forward to the next 50 years" A talk by the Chairman	Sussex Room
1430	"New Lines and Logos" - - . . . Presenting a modern image for a new era in the company's history	Sussex Room
1600	Tea and depart	

Task 3.7

Typist: Use A5 paper, with the longer edge at the top.

SKI BARGAINS

Travel to and from Switzerland by air or Andorra by coach and enjoy the fun and thrills of the slopes as well as the lively nightlife. First-class accommodation in our specially selected ski resorts:

<u>Accommodation</u>	<u>7 Nights</u>	<u>14 Nights</u>
Hotel, bed and breakfast	£249	£449
Hotel, half board	£199	£379
Apartment, self catering ↓	£197	£405 ↑
Hotel, half board . . . . . ↓	£189	£399 ↓
Room only, self catering	£89	£299
Room only, self catering	£49	£169
Villa, self catering	£86	£193

Call for more details on 01 930 5115 and ask for our free winter ski and sun brochures for hotel accommodation, or browse through our winter villas and apartments brochure for the best in self catering holidays.

TYPIST: Type on A5 paper with the longer edge at the top.

ACKNOWLEDGEMENTS

The authors would like to express their appreciation of the encouragement, support and forbearance of their husbands, Robert and William, and their sons, Andrew, John and Christopher.

All the items pictured are the work of the authors with the exception of those listed below.

Design	Maker	Photograph
Clamshell tea cosy	Mary Smith	8
Cathedral window cushion	Alison Clare	12
Oak leaf jacket	Bev Swartz	16 B
Blazing star jacket	Anna Seung	16 A
Grape basket quilt	Jane Bell	19
Strip waistcoat	David King	21
Rose garden quilt	Jane Bell	26
Shell wall hanging	Mary Smith	29
Double wedding ring quilt	Jean Rosen	31
Pincushions and sachets	Debbi Duke	35

Task 3.9

Typist: use A5 paper with the longer edge at the top.

PRAXIBIKE CYCLES SUPPLIERS

We at Praxibike Cycles have decided to hold a special end of summer sale to clear some of our vast stock of over 4000 bikes and make more room for our Christmas deliveries. We have slashed some prices by as much as 40%. See below for a few examples.

Description	Wheel Size	Special Price
10-speed with mudguards, rack and stand	24"	£99.95
12-speed exclusive racer	26"	£89.95
12-speed fully equipped super racer	26"	£129.95
12-speed long distance racer	26"	£159.95
12-speed long distance racer	24"	£135.95
Special stunt cycle	20"	£89.95
Super mountain bike	20"	£99.95
Top quality stunt cycle	20"	£69.95
12-speed road cycle	26"	£99.95

Task 3.10

(A5 paper with the shorter edge at the top)

DISCONTINUED LINES AT SPECIALLY REDUCED PRICES

These offers are only available while stocks last. Order on a standard order form, quoting the code numbers given below. Please add £1 to your order towards the cost of postage and packing. All cards have 3 panels with aperture shape as stated; envelopes not included.

Code	Description	Price Each
DL001	Beige card, white line, oblong	13p
DL002	Beige card, oval	13p
DL003	Pink card, white line, square . . .	10p
DL005	Green card, circle	9p
DL004	Plain white card, oblong . . .	10p
DL006	Apricot card, circle . . .	9p
DL007	Cream card, brown border, square	9p
DL008	Apricot card, oval . . .	8p
DL009	Olive card, square	8p

4 Typed drafts for correction

Notes to candidates

Practice for this type of task starts overleaf, on page 34. In the exams there are always handwritten corrections in these typed drafts. In addition, some of the typed words have circles, to call your attention to errors. You must read the surrounding words or sentences to see what is wrong with each of the circled words. You will then be able to ensure your typed version contains accurate corrections of the errors. Circles may also call attention to errors in linespacing and punctuation which must be corrected.

Aim to type, check and correct this type of task within 20 minutes. 00.20

Task 4.1

Please key the text below to fit on plain A4 paper. Correct the mistakes in the circled words and make any other changes shown.

MUSIC WITH PICTURES

Compact discs were launched in March 1983 and ~~only just over 5 years on~~ the next step has now emerged in the form of COMPACT DISC VIDEO.

The new format requires the (purchase) of a new ~~kind~~ type of player. It ~~is certain to question the relationship~~ may change the use of television and audio in the home.

Popular video (disc's) will have 5 (mintues) of pictures and about 20 minutes of sound. (Othwr) types of disc will be the same size as a long playing record with a playing time of up to 2 hours.

The first issues include

1 "Bad" by Michael Jackson
2 "The Witches of Eastwick"
3 "Salome"

Change to double line spacing

In its popular form it ~~gives pictures and sound of very high quality and~~ is quite thrilling. It (look) and sounds good and is fairly cheap to buy. Discs of other types of (musuc) and of films ~~are likely to be much more expensive.~~ tend to be dearer. [A player will play both audio and video discs. (p)layers and discs are in the shops now.

Sell at around £500 and will

Leave 3 clear line spaces

Your local stockist is:

Midway Records
(Manager: Mr John Green)
Derby Lane
Poole
Dorset
BH92 4AX

Task 4.2

Key this text to fit on an A4 sheet of plain paper. Use double line spacing except where instructed otherwise. Correct the circled errors and make any other changes shown.

NOTICE TO ALL STAFF

Welcome back to college! [The start of a new year is always an exciting time and our student numbers this year ~~on both full-time and part-time courses~~ are well up on those for the last academic year. ~~Funds can be something of an annual~~ Money is still a bit of a problem when it comes to funding for courses but we are making good headway in this field.

NEW COURSES for this year are:

a) Hair and Beauty Care - Tutor: Mary Jones
b) Desk Top Publishimg - Tutor: Kashmir Singh
c) Modern Office Skills - Tytor: Eric Morgan

(Single line spacing)

There is still a few places on these courses and ~~if anyone is interested they~~ anyone who shows an interest should be referred to the tutor .concerned.

The college bookshop will open again next Minday and orders for class set's of books may be placed from that day.

the canteen is once again open to students and staff ~~for meals and snacks throughout the day~~ and will now ~~provide~~ offer a selection of ethnic food as well as the fare that has been on offer in the past.

I wish you all a good year.

(Leave 4 clear line spaces)

Principal

Task 4.3

Key this text, for A4 plain paper.
Some words have rings round all or part of them to indicate keyboarding errors. Please correct them and make any other changes needed.

Market Day in Gloston   a tiny village tucked away

Gloston is in the Clifton Hills. Pass through it any day of the week except Thursday and it seems ~~no different from any other village.~~ Thursday, However, is market day. // The Gloston Market is famous for 3 things.   in no way out of the ordinary.

1 Cheese

More than 100 types of cheese ~~from every cheese-producing country in the world~~ is to be found on Mrs Charter's chesse stall. Many of them are rare and ~~all~~ ~~most~~ are delicious.

2 Country Wines

Max Smiths home fermented cuontry wines are ~~without any shadow of a doubt~~ the best in the region. They can only be bought at the Gloston Markit. He ~~has always refused to sell to~~ the wine trade.   does not supply

3 Black Pudding

Janet Townsend's black pudding is famous - she wun a prize for it in the "Boudin Noir competition in France. People come from far and wide to make a purchase from her.

leave at least 12 clear line spaces

Gloston Market opens at 8.30 am each Thursday (except for Christmas week) and carries on trading until 6.00 pm.

When visiting the region, make sure not to miss it.

The numbered paragraphs should be in double line spacing.

Task 4.4

Key in the text below – it will need to go on A4 plain paper. The circles indicate keyboarding mistakes. Please correct them and make the other changes indicated.

LAMB CHOP PARCELS WITH MUSHROOMS AND YOGHURT

Here is a easy and quick recipe for cooking lamb chops with very litkle mess and a result that is guaranteed (CAPS) to please your guests.

Cooking can be done ~~by following the three stages~~ in three steps as shown below. heat the oven to Regulo 4 first.

(Double line spacing)

1 Line a baking tin with cooking foil. Allow one chip per person and brown the chops ~~all over on the top of the cooker~~ in melted butter in a frying pan.

Season them with salt, freshly ground black pepper and thyme.

2 Chop some mushrooms ~~coarsely~~ finely and ~~soften them in hot oil~~ cook in the same butter until soft. Add the juice of half a lemons and sizzle for a minute. Stir in one tablespoonful of flour ~~and mix it well into the mushrooms~~ and spoon this rather sticky mixture over the chops.

3 Pour a tablespoonful of plain yoghurt over each chop and wrap the chop's in the foil. Cook in the oven for one hour and serve at once. This is a rich

recipe, so any vehetables, salads, etc served with the lamb chops should be simply presented.

Please leave 4 clear line spaces above and below the numbered paragraphs

Task 4.5

The following is to be on A4 plain paper. Circled words and circles in the text indicate errors. Please correct them and make all the other changes.

Burton Software plc, ~~a known market leader in software~~ who have organised this year's software show, annuonce that ~~with effect from next season~~ from next year the show will be held three time a year.

The spring show will take place during May at Wembley, where it will expand to occupy the Woolwich Hall.

This is as a result of rapid sales of floorspace for this year's event.

The summer show also will be held at Wembley, in July and August, but it will be in the Godolphin Hall // The final sgow of the year will be held at the Natoinal Exhibition Centre. ~~This is situated near Birmingham International Airport.~~ It will take place during October.

Dates for next years shows are as follows:

Double line spacing

1) Spring: 14 - 20 May
2) Summer: 28 July - 10 August
3) Winter: 16 - 25 October.

Further ~~details of~~ ~~information about~~ the above shows, giving information about travel, times, tickets etc ~~are easily obtained by applying~~ may be obtained by writing to:

Ms Joy Adams, Burton Software plc, Stansted House, Mere Lane, Sutton Coldfield, West Midlands

or telephoning her on: 021-397 8096.

Leave 3 clear line spaces

LOOK FORWARD TO SEEING YOU AT ONE OF THE SHOWS!

Task 4.6

Key in this information sheet to go on A4 plain paper, correcting the circled words. Your second paragraph should be in double line spacing, and the rest of the text should be in single line spacing. Leave 3 clear line spaces above and below the numbered paragraphs.

"HOW TO DRIVE A COMPUTER"

If you buy an IBM or IBM compatible machine today, you ~~ought to~~ really need to know a bit about ~~be familiar with the commands in~~ DOS. DOS stand's for disk operating system This is the sustem that is to be found on the "boot" or "system" disk supplied with the machine and which you ~~insert at the beginning of a session and~~ use to start the machine.

There are a number of commands in DOS that will prove very useful.

Perhaps the three that you will find yourslef using most often are those listed below.

1 FORMAT

This command will give a brand new disk the number of tracks and sectors you need for the drive you use to format the disk.

2 COPY

This command will enabble you to ~~make copies of files on the same disk and~~ copy files saved on one disk onto a second disk without losing the originals.

3 DIR

This command will display a lists of all ~~records~~ files in the drive that the machine is "reading".

To find out more about DOS, ~~attend one of the sessions~~ book a place on our "How to drive a computer" course.

Task 4.7

Please key in the text shown below.
It needs to go on plain A4 paper.
Use double line spacing except for the numbered items, as indicated. Correct all errors, including those in the circled words.

COMBINE - AN INTEGRATED PACKAGE

Leave 8 line spaces here please

This is a package that include 3 of the most popular types of software, namely word processing, data base and spreadsheet. They can be combonedin a variety of different ways to make it very simple for the user to achieve complex targets.

The 3 parts of the paclage are:

1) SCRIPT - the word processor,
2) FILE - the data base, and
3) PLAN - the spreadsheet.

Single line spacing

Text can be keyed in using "Script" and saved in the normal way. Records can be entered into "File" and ~~these may be incorporated into~~ can then be combined with a "Script" file to prokuce a simple mailshot. Statistical data can be entered onto the "Plan" spreadsheet and ~~it is very simple to give a command so that any~~ series of figures can then be changed into a graph. // Data can be taken from a graph or spreadsheet and then inserted into a "Script" file. In this way the ~~operator~~ user can produce a printout that look's as though it has been keyyed in by a trained operator.

the fact is that ~~this product is very simply~~ the package can be mastered by a complete beginner in under 2 hours!

Task 4.8

Type or word process this text to fit on plain A4. Use single line spacing, except where instructed otherwise.

<u>Desk Top Publishing</u> *Leave 3 clear line spaces*

What is desk top publishing? Broadly, it is a method of keying in graphics and text using a computer screen and keybaord. These are then organised to produce a printed copy. In the past this would have ~~required the expertise of someone~~ *had to be designed* using the tools of the printing trade.

In other words, it is a system which takes text files and combine them on screen with piccture files into a page layout. The final printouts ~~that are produced using this sort of program~~ have a very professional look and cost only a fraction of the price ~~it would be necessary for you~~ *you might have* to pay an artwork studio or printer.

There are many use's to which it can be put, eg:

a) NEWS-SHEETS,
b) MENUS,
c) BROCHURES.

Double line spacing

The beauty ~~of a desk top publishing system~~ is that it does not require any special keyboard skills.

The text can be word prosessed by one person, *the graphics designed by a second* and the page organised by the desk top publisher who makes any changes ~~needed~~ *necessary* using a mouse" to move things around the page.

Circles around all or part of a word indicate keyboarding mistakes. Please correct them.

Task 4.9

Leave 4 line spaces here

and lessons cost £10 each,

LEARNING TO DRIVE

Many people think that learning to drive is a simple thing to do. however, as you get older, it become more difficult.

Some say you need one lesson for every year of your life. Just thonk, if you start learning at 40 it could cost you £400 before you pass your test! If you ARE thinking of ~~starting to have driving lessons~~ learning to drive, here are some tip's.

Double line spacing

a) Take your leesons fairly early in the day as you will be fresher then and able to ~~handle the car with more care and~~ concentrate better.

b) Have at least 2 lessons a week to make sure you ~~maintain some familiarity with the vehicle~~ remain familiar with the car you are learning in.

c) Get ~~plenty~~ lots of practice in another car, with someone who is able to remain calm with a learner driver!

When you ~~finally have the confidence and ability to~~ pass your test, remenber not to go mad! After all, until then other drivers could see that you were a laerner. In a way you are still but now they have no way of telling.

Key in the above text making the changes shown and correcting the circled words. Make sure it will fit on plain A4 paper.

Task 4.10

Key in this text to go on A4 plain paper. Change to single line spacing except for the lettered paragraphs. Correct the circled words, and make the other changes shown.

6 clear line spaces here please

Country Discovery

Take your car and spend time away ~~from the pressures and stresses of work~~ in delightful rural Hampshire.

With ~~the emphasis on getting right away~~ peace and quiet very much in mind you can stay or tour for 2 or 3 nights in one of our inns. each has such a warmth of atmosphere and welcome that you will feal like a valued guest from the moment you check in.

Our prices are ~~quite~~ very competitive - just look.

a) Little Inn, Liphook - £46 per person for 2 nights, £15 for each extra night.

b) The Welcome Inn, Bosham - £50 per person for 2 niggts, £18 for each extra night.

c) Inn of Delight, Cadnam - £52 per person for 2 nights, £19 for each extra night.

Our prices includes full english breakfast and room with bath, shower and wc. Visits to local beauty spot's ~~and areas of outstanding local interest~~ will be recommended by your host and in adition free maps of the area are provided. [Why not book your COUNTRY DISCOVERY break now? Take time off to relax and ~~find yourself going back to work~~ you will return home refreshed and rested.

5 Forms for completion

Notes to candidates

In the Stage I exam, as in this book, details are given in the same order as the headings in the pre-printed form. Sometimes, the details are written on a copy of the form, ready for you to copy eg Task 5.3.

Don't forget to make any deletions clearly. Do not sign the forms you type.

RSA forms for typing the tasks in this book are available from bookshops, or, if you have difficulty, contact the Publishers. In the exam, you will be provided with two copies of the form for Task 6 in case you spoil your first attempt.

Aim to type, check and correct this type of task within 5 minutes. 00.05

Task 5.1

Miss Lucas
6 Inchcombe Street
SHEFFIELD
Yorkshire
S38 9DM

(Complete the Order Form for Studio Prints Ltd. You may type all entries in capitals if you wish.)

2A	18 mm × 26 mm	3
6	13 mm × 18 mm	4
8B	28 mm × 36 mm	1

Task 5.2

Mrs Jean Andrews
75 Manning Drive
LEICESTER
LE1 6TN

(TYPIST: Please complete the Studio Prints Ltd Order form. You may type all entries in capitals if you wish.)

PROOF NUMBER	SIZE	NUMBER REQUIRED
A/23	20 cm × 25 cm	One
A/24	30 cm × 25 cm	Two
A/16	20 cm × 25 cm	Six

Task 5.3

Type the following details using the form

You may type all entries in capitals if you wish

TRUSTON COMPREHENSIVE SCHOOL

PUPIL'S PART-TIME EMPLOYMENT

Name of Pupil .... Keith Watson ....

Name of Employer .... Mrs Craig ....

Address .... Martins (Chemists) ....

.... 6 The Parade ....

.... TRUSTON ....

Telephone No .... 469824 ....

Business .... Chemist ....

Nature of Employment .... Stacking shelves ....

HOURS OF EMPLOYMENT

Monday		to	
Tuesday		to	
Wednesday		to	
Thursday		to	
Friday		to	
Saturday	8 am	to	12 noon
Lunch Period		to	
Total Hours		4	

Signature ....

* ~~Manager/Supervisor~~/Tutor

Date ....

* delete as appropriate

Task 5.4

TYPIST: Please complete the Pupil's Part-time Employment form. You may type all entries in capitals if you wish.

Name of Pupil Catherine Kane

Name of Employer Justifica Gowns

Address Benchford Drive
NOTTINGHAM
NG1 3SL

Telephone No 0602 735641

Business Boutique

Nature of Employment Sales Assistant

HOURS OF EMPLOYMENT

Saturday 8.30 am to 5.30 pm

Total Hours 9

Tutor to sign the form.

Task 5.5

TYPIST: Complete the Villiers Order Form. You may type all entries in capitals if you wish.

ORDER No. 254

To Praxiteles Group
8 John Adam Street
LONDON
WC2N 6EZ

CODE NO	QTY	DESCRIPTION	UNIT PRICE £	PRICE £ p
QRS/2789	1	Oil Pressure Gauge	9.00	9.00
			TOTAL	£9.00

Task 5.6

TYPIST: Complete the Villiers Order Form. You may type all entries in capitals if you wish.

Order No 927

To John Draper Plumbing Limited
28 Richard Avenue
YORK
YO1 3PA

CODE No	QTY	DESCRIPTION	UNIT PRICE £	PRICE £ p
Z/1562	2	Brass Taps	5.00	10.00
			TOTAL	£10.00

Task 5.7

Complete form the Order as follows. You may type all entries in capitals if you wish

ORDER

ORDER NO. 15827

VILLIERS ENGINEERING

25 GREEN STREET

LONDON NW4 6XL

TO

MS J SMITHSON
18 PARK AVE.
BRACKNELL
BERKS
RG23 6MY

DATE

CODE NO.	QTY.	DESCRIPTION	UNIT PRICE £	PRICE £	PRICE p
PX004	2	FILING CABINETS	95.15	190	30
			TOTAL £	190	30

SIGNED

FOR EXPORT

Task 5.8

Complete the Villiers Order Form

You may type all entries in capitals if you wish.

ORDER NO. 25/89

To Mr Tim Mason
6a Ludlow Gardens
ROMFORD
Essex RM6 1LP

ME538	1	Lawn Mower	59.99	59.99
		Total		59.99

Task 5.9

PRAXITELES INSURANCE GROUP

PRAXITELES HOUSE · ADAM STREET · LONDON WC2N 6EZ
TELEPHONE 01 930 5115

To

JAMES RUSSELL ESQ
9 SPUR ROAD
BRIDGNORTH
SHROPSHIRE
WV29 6ML

Date:

Policy Number: H20095/156A

Insured: JAMES RUSSELL

Premium: £126.84

Effective Date: 1 May 1989

Please refer to sections 2 and 6 below.

1 ☐ We confirm that cover has now ceased and the time on risk charge is as shown above.

2 ☒ Amendments noted. No revised document(s) necessary. Premium adjustment is as shown above.

3 ☐ Amendments noted. Revised document(s) attached. Premium adjustment is as shown above.

4 ☐ Duplicate document(s) attached.

5 ☐ Policy cancelled. Return document is as shown above.

6 ☒ Please remit the premium shown above without delay.

7 ☐

Type these details on the form.

You may type all entries in capitals if you wish

Task 5.10

TYPIST: Please complete the Car Parking Permits form. You may type all entries in capitals if you wish.

NAME: Angela Maltby

DEPARTMENT CODE: P/5

I do drive to work.

REGULAR VEHICLE	Make and Model	Vauxhall Cavalier
	Registration No	D125 WAV
	Colour	Sapphire Blue
SECOND VEHICLE	Make and Model	Ford Fiesta
	Registration No	BJU 963Y
	Colour	Polar White

USUAL CAR PARK: Administration Block

Worked examples

1 Letters and memos

Task 1.1

PRAXITELES GROUP

A fictitious organisation for examination purposes only

PRAXITELES HOUSE · ADAM STREET · LONDON WC2N 6EZ
TELEPHONE 01 930 5115

Our ref BD/433

Your ref

(Date of typing)

Mrs Janet Moores
Moores & Evans plc
LOWER CLIFTON
Worcs
WR12 6EQ

Dear Mrs Moores

PRAXITELES OPERA GROUP

Your two sets of complimentary opera tickets are enclosed.

The works being performed are MEDEA by Cherubini and ALBERT HERRING by Britten. I believe that these will be the first performances of both works in this region.

Those taking the major roles are:

Mary Golding as Medea,
Norman Reid as Jason,
Mike Bishop as Albert,
Daphne Lane as Lady Billows.

If you should require any more tickets please contact the secretary of the opera group. Seat prices are £7.50 and £5.00. There is a 10% discount for party bookings of 15 or more. As a sponsor of the opera group you will receive free programmes. Please collect these from the box office on arrival.

I am sure that you and your guests will enjoy these very different works. The one is high tragedy and the other is a comedy. I very much look forward to meeting you and your guests.

Yours sincerely
Praxiteles Group

Barbara Davis
Group Secretary

Encs

(carbon copy)

Mrs Janet Moores
Moores & Evans plc
LOWER CLIFTON
Worcs
WR12 6EQ

Task 1.2

MEMORANDUM

From	Jane Fellows	*Ref*	JF/POG
To	Barbara Davis	*Date*	(Date of typing)

URGENT

Opera Plot Outlines

Below are plot outlines of the two works being performed this year. I think these should definitely be added to the cast lists. The company is giving these to all employees coming next Tuesday and Thursday to the dress rehearsals.

"Medea is a Greek sorceress. Her husband Jason leaves her and she kills his children and new wife in revenge.

"Albert Herring is crowned King of the May. He spends his prize money on drinking and debauchery that night. This helps free him from his nagging mother."

I would be very grateful if this could be done today as the cast lists are ready for printing.

Programmes for both operas have now been printed and copies for sponsors will be sent up to you. These are to be left at the box office.

Task 1.3

PRAXITELES GROUP

A fictitious organisation for examination purposes only

PRAXITELES HOUSE · ADAM STREET · LONDON WC2N 6EZ

TELEPHONE 01 930 5115

Our ref SA/LC/88

Your ref

(Date of typing)

Miss Louise Cooke
21 Calverton Crescent
Brampton Bierlow
ROTHERHAM
South Yorkshire
S62 3QP

Dear Miss Cooke

Service Agreement - Vauxhall Nova

Congratulations on choosing to buy one of our cars. You will get many hours of pleasure and safe motoring from this car.

The main ingredient for safe motoring is regular servicing. The makers recommend a service every 12 months or 9,000 miles. Michael Oliver, our senior salesman, should already have told you about these limits at the time of the sale. He should also have given you a catalogue. The catalogue shows the benefits of our Fixed Price Service programme.

The manufacturers have approved service limits for this model. To benefit from your breakdown insurance you must keep within these limits. There is an allowable leeway of 700 miles or 14 days either side of the agreed mileage and time periods.

The policy may be CANCELLED if these limits are not met.

In closing, it is the sole aim of our team to ensure that this deal is only the start of a long association. I hope that you will consider us for your future car purchases.

Yours sincerely

James Powers
General Sales Manager

(carbon copy)

Miss Louise Cooke
21 Calverton Crescent
Brampton Bierlow
ROTHERHAM
South Yorkshire
S62 3QP

Task 1.4

MEMORANDUM

From James Powers
General Sales Manager

Ref SA/LC/88

To John Porter
Service Department

Date (Date of typing)

URGENT

Service Agreement - Vauxhall Nova

You will see from the attached letter that Miss Louise Cooke has taken out our fully extended mechanical breakdown insurance in respect of her Vauxhall Nova car. This should take effect from the time and day of purchase.

However, she wishes to have her car serviced at her local garage instead of at our workshop. I have referred this to Mr Key, our Managing Director, for his review. I feel that in order to guarantee the insurance cover Miss Cooke should have her car checked with us. I will let you know the outcome of my letter to Mr Key.

Enc

Task 1.5

MEMORANDUM

From Tony Stone   *Ref* TS/BVR

To Angela Robson   *Date* (Date of typing)

FRANKFURT CAR STUDY

You will by now have received a copy of the letter which we are about to send out to all those taking part in the above project who live in the south-east region. The tickets and itinerary details should be sent out early next week.

I would remind you that you must have a cheque for £25 ready for each passenger on arrival at Gatwick. These cheques are to pay for travelling expenses and parking fees. On the last trip these cheques were not to hand when we arrived back at the home airport. This time they must all be ready before the passengers leave the airport for their homes. Make sure that you thank each one individually for their help in this very important project.

Task 1.6

PRAXITELES GROUP

A fictitious organisation for examination purposes only

PRAXITELES HOUSE · ADAM STREET · LONDON WC2N 6EZ
TELEPHONE 01 930 5115

Our ref TS/BVR

Your ref

PERSONAL

(Date of typing)

Mrs Stella Rowe
The Warden
6 Saxton Court
EAST GRINSTEAD
Sussex
RH29 3BY

Dear Mrs Rowe

FRANKFURT CAR STUDY

Praxi Research is a British market research agency. It carries out surveys for government departments and leading business concerns. At present we are working on a study in Frankfurt.

Thank you for helping us with this new project. Our purpose is to get the opinions of owners about certain new cars. We hope that you will treat this as an opportunity to pass on your views to the manufacturers about their products.

The study takes the form of a motor show at which you will be asked to fill in a form giving your views on the new cars.

No one will try to sell you anything, either now or later, as a result of this.

You will leave Gatwick Airport at 8.00 am.
The flight will take about two hours.
The return flight will leave at 2.30 pm.

Enclosed are some further details. We feel sure that you will have an interesting and rewarding day.

Yours sincerely
TONY STONE

FIELD DIRECTOR

Enc

(carbon copy)

PERSONAL

Mrs Stella Rowe
The Warden
6 Saxton Court
EAST GRINSTEAD
Sussex
RH29 3BY

Task 1.7

PRAXITELES GROUP

A fictitious organisation for examination purposes only

PRAXITELES HOUSE · ADAM STREET · LONDON WC2N 6EZ

TELEPHONE 01 930 5115

Our ref CLTY/234

Your ref

(Date of typing)

URGENT

Miss Rita Jackson
21 Lavender Close
LEAMINGTON SPA
Warwickshire
CV31 9EA

Dear Miss Jackson

Post of Clerk Typist - Purchasing Department

I acknowledge receipt of your letter of application dated yesterday for the above post. I have had many suitable replies. I would like to start interviewing during the next week. I have arranged the following appointment for you:

TUESDAY of next week at 10.30 am.

If either the date or the time is awkward would you please contact my secretary, Miss Jane Landers, as soon as possible. She will then allot a new time which will suit you and still fit in with my time schedule.

I would be grateful if you would bring along your certificates. You will be required to take a short typing test. The test may be taken on a manual or electronic machine.

After the first talk and test you may be asked to attend our medical office to undergo a full medical. In order to reduce the time involved for this medical would you please complete the enclosed form and bring it with you.

Yours sincerely

David Harrison
PERSONNEL MANAGER

Enc

(carbon copy)

URGENT

Miss Rita Jackson
21 Lavender Close
LEAMINGTON SPA
Warwickshire
CV31 9EA

Task 1.8

MEMORANDUM

From David Harrison
Personnel

To Dr Janet Munro
Medical

Ref CLTY/234

Date (Date of typing)

Post of Clerk Typist - Purchasing Department

I have arranged to see all the suitable applicants for the above post during next week. I believe that the best time for you to conduct the medicals is after lunch. However, I am not able to see everyone in the afternoon. Most of the interviews are planned for 2.30 pm but three are for 10.30 am.

I am sending a medical form to each applicant with a request to complete the form and bring it to the interview. As each person arrives, I will get my secretary to let you have the form straight away. You will then have enough time to study it.

Task 1.9

MEMORANDUM

From	Publicity Manager	*Ref*	TJ/CD
To	Accounts	*Date*	(Date of typing)

EXPENSE ACCOUNTS

I enclose a list of my expenses incurred during my business trip to Germany. I have obtained receipts for the majority of my expenses. I have not claimed for travelling to and from the airport because a chauffeur was provided.

As you can see from the list, the amount is considerable and I would appreciate immediate refund of this money. Perhaps in future I could be allowed to have an advance in respect of expenses to be incurred. I look forward to hearing your views on this request.

Enc

Task 1.10

PRAXITELES GROUP

A fictitious organisation for examination purposes only

PRAXITELES HOUSE · ADAM STREET · LONDON WC2N 6EZ
TELEPHONE 01 930 5115

Our ref GM/GLD

Your ref

(Date of typing)

URGENT

Mr J Brough
12 Midway Close
LEICESTER
LE1 7RJ

Dear Sir

I am writing to confirm the arrangements for the meeting with the clients. This will take place at their offices on Friday 28 May at 10.15 am. I have asked the clients to let me know in which room the meeting is to be held. I will contact you again when this data is to hand.

I understand that the clients would like to have a hint of your findings. They would like the opportunity of making comments prior to the final preparation of your report. The clients are particularly keen to have this meeting because they differ with certain of Mr Hooley's comments about the roofs. We did, of course, briefly discusss this on the phone a little while ago.

A meeting has been arranged with the members of the Council for 11 June. If possible, the Council would like your report to be available for discussion. The Council has requested 3 dozen copies of your report.

> Will it be possible to produce this number?
> Will your report include reference to photographs?

If so, do you think it would be better to have 3 or 4 separate sets of photographs, rather than to produce 3 dozen sets? I would be grateful for your comments in this respect.

I look forward to hearing from you.

Yours faithfully

Gerald Mortison

(carbon copy)

URGENT

Mr J Brough
12 Midway Close
LEICESTER
LE1 7RJ

Task 1.11

PRAXITELES GROUP

A fictitious organisation for examination purposes only

PRAXITELES HOUSE · ADAM STREET · LONDON WC2N 6EZ

TELEPHONE 01 930 5115

Our ref P3/PH/VK

Your ref

(Date of typing)

PERSONAL

Dr and Mrs Robert Binns
Peppercorn Cottage
Alrewas Road
NOTTINGHAM
NG2 4VX

Dear Dr and Mrs Binns

I am writing to offer you, as valued customers, the opportunity to take out a Praxiloan of up to £3,000 to spend on almost anything you like.

A Praxiloan means that you can put your ideas into action NOW. You can spread the loan over any period to suit you from one to five years.

If you borrow £3,000 over one year your repayments will be around £275 per month. For the same amount over five years you will pay £75 monthly.

For peace of mind your repayments can be covered with our own safeguard scheme for only a modest extra charge. This scheme ensures that in the events of illness, accident or even unemployment your repayments will be made for you.

APPLY for your Praxiloan NOW!

To arrange your loan, complete and return the enclosed application form as soon as possible.

If you let us know when you need the money we will make the funds immediately ready for your use.

Yours sincerely

Peter Howard
Loans Manager

Enc

(carbon copy)

PERSONAL

Dr and Mrs Robert Binns
Peppercorn Cottage
Alrewas Road
NOTTINGHAM
NG2 4VX

Task 1.12

MEMORANDUM

From Peter Howard

Ref PH/VK

To Gail Wright
Personal Loans Department

Date (Date of typing)

Advertising Campaign

I have instructed that all members on our books are sent the necessary papers inviting them to apply for a loan. I believe that many requests will come from people wishing to book a holiday abroad. We have sufficient funds at the moment to finance 25 such loans.

All applications from students for temporary loans should be considered with care. You must judge each case on its own merit. However, I must ask you to ensure that students are capable of making regular payments. I suggest you make Charlotte Worthing responsible for vetting all requests.

Members of staff do not qualify to apply for the Praxiloan on offer. Alternative arrangements are being made for staff and will be disclosed shortly.

Task 1.13

MEMORANDUM

From Personnel Manager

Ref KL/EN

To All members of staff

Date (Date of typing)

CUTTING COMMUTING COSTS

I believe that the majority of our staff use public transport to travel to and from work. They know that buying an annual season ticket could save them money. I acknowledge that the initial cost of making such a saving can be formidable.

I have discussed this with other senior members of staff. We have agreed to recommend that the company should consider a scheme whereby loans can be made available. Loans would be at a fixed interest rate. This would be lower than the current rate.

The enclosed table gives examples. I emphasise that the amount payable would not change if interest rates went up or down.

This concession would not apply to temporary staff.

The sum representing your loan plus the interest would be added together and then divided by 12. The answer gives your final monthly replayments.

To qualify, you need to be 18 years of age or over.

If you are interested, please let me know by the end of the week.

Enc

Task 1.14

PRAXITELES GROUP

A fictitious organisation for examination purposes only

PRAXITELES HOUSE · ADAM STREET · LONDON WC2N 6EZ

TELEPHONE 01 930 5115

Our ref ST/ACM

Your ref

PRIVATE

(Date of typing)

Miss Veronica Baxter
6 Woburn Hill
CIRENCESTER
Glos
GL7 15KY

Dear Miss Baxter

ACCOUNT NUMBER B42976V

Many of our cardholders have found that the credit limits on their cards are now too low for their needs. They have written to ask for an increase. For this reason we have reviewed our limits for all our cardholders.

To try to ensure that we meet our customers' needs, we have chosen certain accounts where a higher limit would appear to be appropriate.

> As a result your own limit has been increased to £950. This takes immediate effect. We do hope that you will find this extra credit helpful.

I am sure you agree that using your Proxicard is a safer method of paying for goods than carrying cash or cheques in your wallet or handbag.

Yours sincerely
Stephen Turner

PRAXICARD CHIEF EXECUTIVE

(carbon copy)

PRIVATE

Miss Veronica Baxter
6 Woburn Hill
CIRENCESTER
Glos
GL7 15KY

Task 1.15

PRAXITELES GROUP

A fictitious organisation for examination purposes only

PRAXITELES HOUSE · ADAM STREET · LONDON WC2N 6EZ
TELEPHONE 01 930 5115

Our ref C/92805

Your ref

(Date of typing)

Mr Leonard Coleman
18 Richmond Avenue
BRISTOL
BS28 4BW

Dear Mr Coleman

ORDER C/92805

Thank you for your recent order which was received today. I am very sorry to have to write to tell you that I have to delay this order.

I have referred to the electoral register. I believe that it may be that an error has been made in the detail of your address. I am, of course, concerned in case such an error should result in the goods being sent to the wrong address.

Will you please confirm that the following statements are correct.

The above address is correct.

You have lived there at least a year.

If either of these statements is incorrect, please let me know. If you have moved recently, please give me full details of your previous address.

I apologise most sincerely for any inconvenience caused to you. I hope you appreciate that it is necessary that we take precautions to ensure that such a valuable order does not go astray.

A stamped addressed envelope is enclosed.

Yours sincerely
LILIAN BONNER

Praxi Consumer Services Manager

Enc

(Carbon copy)

Mr Leonard Coleman

18 Richmond Avenue

BRISTOL   BS28 4BW

Task 1.16

MEMORANDUM

From Despatch Department *Ref* C/92805

To Customer Services *Date* (Date of typing)

URGENT

I set out below details of a new customer.

Mr Leonard Coleman
18 Richmond Avenue
BRISTOL
BS28 4BW

It is necessary for a check to be made on this address. It does not appear on the electoral register. Only numbers 2 to 16 are listed.

This is in a new housing area. It may be that it was once a showhome which has now been sold.

If the address proves to be genuine, we can assume that Mr Coleman moved less than a year ago. If so, we will need details of his previous address.

You will no doubt remember there have been occasions when goods have been ordered and sent to an empty house. The keys had been obtained from the selling agents. We are therefore checking on all orders over the value of £100.

Task 1.17

MEMORANDUM

From James Foster, Praxi Investment Department Manager *Ref* JF/DR

To Branch Managers *Date* (Date of typing)

J PLUS BONDS

You will by now have had details of the new J PLUS BONDS. I am hoping that most of these will be taken up by members of Praxi Plus Fund. I have been in touch with all holders of shares in this fund. All such clients should by now have had a leaflet on J Plus. I am hoping that this will lead to a considerable number of enquiries over the next few months.

A supply of the leaflets is being sent to you under separate cover today.

I would remind you to take every opportunity to promote these bonds. If these are not suitable for the purpose, offer the alternative of our current monthly income bonds.

Task 1.18

PRAXITELES GROUP

A fictitious organisation for examination purposes only

PRAXITELES HOUSE · ADAM STREET · LONDON WC2N 6EZ

TELEPHONE 01 930 5115

Our ref JF/DR

Your ref

CONFIDENTIAL

(Date of typing)

Mrs Karen Howard
13 Royston Street
STOCKPORT
Cheshire
SK3 19CZ

Dear Mrs Howard

PRAXI PLUS FUND

The Praxi Plus Fund account which you opened with us just under 5 years ago will mature at the end of next month. My main purpose in writing to you today is to thank you for your support during that time. I would also like to tell you what will happen when the account matures.

You do not have to take any immediate action. All you have to do is call at your local office. This visit should take place before the end of next month. The branch manager or any member cf the staff will be pleased to help you.

A leaflet telling you about our newest fund is enclosed. The rate is high.

> Included is a guarantee of the high differential for the full term of 24 months.

Our local staff will be pleased to discuss details with you. It is not necessary for you to make an appointment. Once again, thank you for your support which I do hope will continue.

Yours sincerely
JAMES FOSTER

Praxi Investment Department Manager

Enc

(carbon copy)

CONFIDENTIAL

Mrs Karen Howard
13 Royston Street
STOCKPORT
Cheshire
SK3 19CZ

2 Draft notices for display

Task 2.1

Praxiteles Opera Group

S U M M E R   S E A S O N

This year this opera group is mounting two works. These are "Medea" by Cherubini and "Albert Herring" by Benjamin Britten.

Seat prices are £7.50 and £5.00. There is a 10% reduction for parties (15 or more) and a 50% reduction for children under 13.

Performances are in the Great Hall at Praxiteles House. Praxiteles Opera Group is an amateur company with very high standards. It has been favourably compared with the major opera companies.

The last performance of each work is for charity and all proceeds will go to CHILDREN IN NEED.

Task 2.2

Praxiteles Wildlife Park

O F F E R S

25% off normal admission charges during the winter season, October-March.

LOTS TO SEE AND DO!

Spend a day at Praxiteles Wildlife Park. Visit the reptile house and aquarium. Take a look at the tigers, lions, pumas, bears, elephants, monkeys, penguins, deer and birds. Don't miss the sea-lion show (every day at 1400 hours). Relax in the tropical gardens. Enjoy a meal in our restaurant and try our tea rooms.

Take this opportunity to have a really super day out.

Praxiteles Wildlife Park
Hudson Road
SPARKWELL
Plymouth

Telephone: (0653) 40126

Opening hours: 1000-1800 hours daily.

Task 2.3

Staff Notice

P R A X I T E L E S   S O C I A L   C L U B

SPONSORED BED PUSH

The sponsored bed push held last month raised a grand total of £1001.92 - almost 75% up on last year's total.

Congratulations to all who took part!

Fancy dress prizes were awarded to:

1st Caroline Hold
2nd Peter Edwards.

It has been agreed that 25% of the proceeds should be donated to a local charity. As a result, the Committee would welcome suggestions for a worthwhile local charity to receive a donation of £250.00. Please pass on your ideas to the Club Secretary, Christine Gill.

David Shanks - Chairman
Praxiteles Social Club

Task 2.4

P R A X I   P R O M O T I O N S   P R E S E N T

David and Fred in Concert

The famous rock duo, DAVID AND FRED, will be in town shortly for a series of concerts sponsored by Praxi Records Limited.

They will be signing copies of their album, "David and Fred in Concert", at Praxi House on Friday of next week from 9.30 am - 11.30 am and 2.30 pm - 4.30 pm. You may also receive signed copies by sending an order with £7.50 for the black disc or £12.50 for the compact disc. Prices include postage.

Address your orders to:

Praxi Records Limited
Praxi House
Adam Street
LONDON
WC2N 6EZ

Task 2.5

PRAXITELES FOTO STUDIO

proudly announces the opening of its new branch

at

101 St Mary's Road
HULL
HU1 2NP

Allow Praxiteles Foto Studio to help you capture those special moments on film forever:

weddings
baby portraits
anniversaries.

S P E C I A L   O F F E R

<u>Portrait Sitting</u>

Sitting fee £25

Order from mounted slides, colour prints in a variety of sizes, complete with presentation folders and receive absolutely <u>free</u>, one large print, 250 mm x 175 mm.

Why not ring us to make an appointment now? Our phone number is (0482) 718901. We are open Monday-Saturday, 10.00 am-4.00 pm. We are pleased to offer free help and advice.

Task 2.6

<u>Praxiteles Textiles plc</u>

V A C A N C Y

SECRETARY TO SALES DIRECTOR

Salary: £10,000 per annum

Age Range: Over 30

Praxiteles Textiles plc is a fast growing company. The Sales Director runs a busy sales office and requires a hard working aide to help him with a heavy work load.

Applicants must have good typing and shorthand skills. A tactful manner and the ability to work under pressure will be essential.

The post offers benefits to the value of approximately £3,000 per annum: private health care, share bonus and pension.

Apply in writing to:

Mrs Anita Chan
Box 25
LEEDS
LS2 4NX

Task 2.7

P R A X I T E L E S   S U N   T O U R S

<u>Hotel Dominque, Neja, Costa del Sol</u>

NOTICE TO CLIENTS

Hello, my name is Sharon.

I am your Praxiteles Sun Tours representative here in the Hotel Dominque.

I am available each day except Sundays (my day off), at my desk in the hotel foyer, between the hours of 9.30-11.45 am. I also hold a happy hour at the poolside bar at midday, Mondays-Saturdays, for all new arrivals.

In my absence please find 2 reference folders and 4 tourist booklets on my desk, which I hope you will find of use.

Regards

SHARON

3 Drafts including tables

Task 3.1

PRAXI FENCING SUPPLIERS

Manufacturers of fencing panels and concrete fencing and garden products.

Save money! Buy direct, with immediate free delivery!

Sample prices given below; other sizes readily available.

Description	Size (feet)	Price
		£
Pine rustic	6 x 6	7.65
Pine rustic	6 x 4	6.80
Closeboard	6 x 6	14.00
Closeboard	6 x 4	19.75
Reinforced concrete posts	9	5.25
Reinforced concrete posts	7	4.10
Wooden posts	8	2.95
Wooden posts	6	2.50
Reinforced concrete gravel boards	6 x 12	3.85
Reinforced concrete gravel boards	6 x 6	2.80
Patio paving slabs, natural	2 x 2	1.65
Patio paving slabs, coloured	2 x 2	1.70

Task 3.2

DO YOU KNOW YOUR ONIONS?

Onions can be sliced, chopped or grated, eaten raw, fried, roasted or pickled. They vary in texture, flavour and strength, and in shape, type and size.

Nutritionally, onions are excellent. Raw globe onions contain 23 calories per 100 g - though fried ones contain 345 calories per 100 g.

Type	Taste	Time to Buy
Globe	Very pungent and strong	November to February
Spanish	Mild, sweet and crisp	July to April
Italian	Mild and sweet	April to May
Silverskins ...	Pungent and strong	September
White	Mild and sweet	September to August
Shallots	Mellow, sweet and delicate	August to October
Spring onions	Mild and delicate	July to August

Task 3.3

FREE FITTING OF ALL OUR TYRES

PRAXITELES TYRE REPLACEMENT

New tyres are adequately speed rated, meeting every European specification; remoulds are subjected to rigorous tests, while part-worn tyres are ideally suitable for the spare wheel.

	Size	Price
Firestone	155 x 12	£15.95
Firestone	175 x 13	£19.50
Firestone	185 x 14	£24.95
Goodyear	145 x 10	£14.75
Goodyear	155 x 13	£20.95
Goodyear	165 x 13	£22.00
Dunlop	145 x 10	£14.70
Dunlop	155 x 13	£20.00
Dunlop	165 x 13	£22.00
Remould	185 x 14	£17.50
Part-worn	175 x 14	£10.90
Part-worn	185 x 14	£11.90

Telephone 01 930 5115

PRAXITELES TYRE REPLACEMENT
Adam Street
London WC2N 6EZ

Task 3.4

PRAXITELES GROUP - CATERING SERVICE

As requested at the last Group board meeting, the accountant has now prepared a summary of cash forecast for the first 3 months of the new trading year. The figures suggest that earlier concern is borne out and steps must be taken to improve matters. The figures will be discussed in detail next week.

	January	February	March
	£,000	£,000	£,000
Total estimated receipts	8,500	11,400	9,800
Total estimated payments	9,000	8,000	14,000
Bank balance at start month	1,000	500	3,900
Excess of receipts over payments (net inflow)		3,400	
Excess of payments over receipts (net outflow)	500		4,200
Bank balance at end month	500	3,900	300 (overdrawn)

Task 3.5

PRAXIGLASS GARDEN POOLS

Bring your garden alive with one of our garden pools. We have developed a new process to create larger, stronger glassfibre pools specially designed to suit every shape and size of garden. Simple to install and guaranteed for 12 years, our pools add charm and magic to your garden.

	Depth	Gallons
Circular	46 cm	100
Square	30 cm	60
Hourglass	51 cm	65
Irregular	51 cm	110
Three-cornered	51 cm	65
Crescent	30 cm	36
Elongated	51 cm	270
Small circular	30 cm	25

To help you decide which pool suits your garden, we have prepared a leaflet illustrating our complete range, including scale drawings for size comparison. Ask for a copy at your nearest garden centre

Task 3.6

PRAXITELES GROUP ANNIVERSARY CONFERENCE

Time	Programme	Venue
1000	"50 years in the market place" .... An illustrated talk by the Sales Director	Sussex Room
1030	"Selling in the Nineties" .... Introduced by John Harper	Sussex Room
1045	Coffee	Lounge
1115	Workshops .... Delegates will be allocated to one of 3 groups	Sussex Room Kent Room Surrey Room
1215	Report back to main meeting .... Followed by question and answer session	Sussex Room
1300	Lunch	Restaurant
1430	"New Lines and Logos" .... Presenting a modern image for a new era in the company's history	Sussex Room
1530	"Looking forward to the next 50 years" .... A talk by the Chairman	Sussex Room
1600	Tea and depart	

Task 3.7

SKI BARGAINS

Travel to and from Switzerland by air or Andorra by coach and enjoy the fun and thrills of the slopes as well as the lively nightlife. First-class accommodation in our specially selected ski resorts:

Accommodation	7 Nights	14 Nights
Hotel, bed and breakfast	£249	£449
Hotel, half board	£199	£379
Hotel, half board	£189	£399
Apartment, self catering	£197	£405
Room only, self catering	£89	£299
Room only, self catering	£49	£169
Villa, self catering ...	£86	£193

Call for more details on 01 930 5115 and ask for our free winter ski and sun brochures for hotel accommodation, or browse through our winter villas and apartments brochure for the best in self catering holidays.

Task 3.8

ACKNOWLEDGEMENTS

The authors would like to express their appreciation of the encouragement, support and forbearance of their husbands, Robert and William, and their sons, Andrew, John and Christopher.

All the items pictured are the work of the authors with the exception of those listed below.

Design	Maker	Photograph
Clamshell tea cosy	Mary Smith	8
Cathedral window cushion	Alison Clare	12
Blazing star jacket	Anna Seung	16A
Oak leaf jacket	Bev Swartz	16B
Grape basket quilt	Jane Bell	19
Strip waistcoat	David King	21
Rose garden quilt	Jane Bell	26
Shell wall hanging	Mary Smith	29
Double wedding ring quilt	Jean Rosen	31
Pincushions and sachets	Debbi Duke	35

Task 3.9

PRAXIBIKE CYCLES SUPPLIERS

We at Praxibike Cycles have decided to hold a special end of summer sale to clear some of our vast stock of over 4000 bikes and make more room for our Christmas deliveries. We have slashed some prices by as much as 40%. See below for a few examples.

Description	Wheel Size	Special Price
10-speed with mudguards, rack and stand	24"	£99.95
12-speed exclusive racer	26"	£89.95
12-speed fully equipped super racer	26"	£129.95
12-speed long distance racer	24"	£135.95
12-speed long distance racer	26"	£159.95
Special stunt cycle	20"	£89.95
Super mountain bike	20"	£99.95
Top quality stunt cycle	20"	£69.95
12-speed road cycle	26"	£99.95

Task 3.10

DISCONTINUED LINES AT SPECIALLY REDUCED PRICES

These offers are only available while stocks last. Order on a standard order form, quoting the code numbers given below. Please add £1 to your order towards the cost of postage and packing. All cards have 3 panels with aperture shape as stated; envelopes not included.

Code	Description	Price Each
DL001	Beige card, white line, oblong	13p
DL002	Beige card, oval	13p
DL003	Pink card, white line, square	10p
DL004	Plain white card, oblong	10p
DL005	Green card, circle	9p
DL006	Apricot card, circle	9p
DL007	Cream card, brown border, square	9p
DL008	Apricot card, oval	8p
DL009	Olive card, square	8p

4 Typed drafts for correction

Task 4.1

MUSIC WITH PICTURES

Compact discs were launched in March 1983 and the next step has now emerged in the form of COMPACT DISC VIDEO. The new format requires the purchase of a new kind of player. It may change the use of television and audio in the home.

Popular video discs will have 5 minutes of pictures and about 20 minutes of sound. Other types of disc will be the same size as a long playing record with a playing time of up to 2 hours.

The first issues include

1 "Bad" by Michael Jackson

2 "The Witches of Eastwick"

3 "Salome"

In its popular form it is quite thrilling. It looks and sounds good and is fairly cheap to buy. Discs of other types of music and of films tend to be dearer.

A player will sell at around £500 and will play both video and audio discs. Players and discs are in the shops now.

Your local stockist is:

Midway Records
(Manager: Mr John Green)
Derby Lane
Poole
Dorset
BH92 4AX

Task 4.2

NOTICE TO ALL STAFF

Welcome back to college!

The start of a new year is always an exciting time and our student numbers this year are well up on those for the last academic year. Money is still a bit of a problem when it comes to funding for courses but we are making good headway in this field.

NEW COURSES for this year are:

a) Hair and Beauty Care - Tutor: Mary Jones
b) Desk Top Publishing - Tutor: Kashmir Singh
c) Modern Office Skills - Tutor: Eric Morgan

There are still a few places on these courses and anyone who shows an interest should be referred to the tutor concerned.

The college bookshop will open again next Monday and orders for class sets of books may be placed from that day. The canteen is once again open to staff and students and will now provide a selection of ethnic food as well as the fare that has been on offer in the past.

Task 4.3

<u>Market Day in Gloston</u>

Gloston is a tiny village tucked away in the Clifton Hills. Pass through it any day of the week except Thursday and it seems in no way out of the ordinary. However, Thursday is market day.

The Gloston Market is famous for 3 things.

1 Cheese

More than 100 types of cheese are to be found on Mrs Charter's cheese stall. Many of them are rare and all are delicious.

2 Country Wines

Max Smith's home fermented country wines are the best in the region. They can only be bought at the Gloston Market. He does not supply the wine trade.

3 Black Pudding

Janet Townsend's black pudding is famous - she won a prize for it in the "Boudin Noir" competition in France. People come from far and wide to make a purchase from her.

Gloston Market opens at 8.30 am each Thursday (except for Christmas week) and carries on trading until 6.00 pm. When visiting the region, make sure not to miss it.

LAMB CHOP PARCELS WITH MUSHROOMS AND YOGHURT

Here is a quick and easy recipe for cooking lamb chops with very little mess and a result that is GUARANTEED to please your guests.

Cooking can be done in 3 steps as shown below. Heat the oven to Regulo 4 first.

1 Line a baking tin with cooking foil. Allow one chop per person and brown the chops in melted butter in a frying pan. Season them with salt, freshly ground black pepper and thyme.

2 Chop some mushrooms coarsely and cook in the same butter until soft. Add the juice of half a lemon and sizzle for a minute. Stir in one tablespoonful of flour and spoon this rather sticky mixture over the chops.

3 Pour a tablespoonful of plain yoghurt over each chop and wrap the chops in the foil. Cook in the oven for one hour and serve at once.

This is a rich recipe, so any vegetables, salads, etc served with the lamb chops should be simply presented.

Task 4.4

Task 4.5

Burton Software plc, who have organised this year's software show, announce that from next year the show will be held three times a year.

The spring show will take place during May at Wembley, where it will expand to occupy the Woolwich Hall. This is as a result of rapid sales of floorspace for this year's event.

The summer show will also be held at Wembley, in July and August, but it will be in the Godolphin Hall

The final show of the year will be held at the National Exhibition Centre. It will take place during October.

Dates for next year's shows are as follows:

1) Spring: 14 - 20 May

2) Summer: 28 July - 10 August

3) Winter: 16 - 25 October.

Further details of the above shows, giving information about travel, times, tickets etc may be obtained by writing to:

Ms Joy Adams, Burton Software plc, Stansted House, Mere Lane, Sutton Coldfield, West Midlands

or telephoning her on: 021-397 8096.

LOOK FORWARD TO SEEING YOU AT ONE OF THE SHOWS!

Task 4.6

"HOW TO DRIVE A COMPUTER"

If you buy an IBM or IBM compatible machine today, you really need to know a bit about DOS.

DOS stands for disk operating system. This is the system that is to be found on the "system" or "boot" disk supplied with the machine and which you use to start the machine.

There are a number of commands in DOS that will prove very useful. Perhaps the three that you will find yourself using most often are those listed below.

1 FORMAT

This command will give a brand new disk the number of tracks and sectors you need for the drive you use to format the disk.

2 COPY

This command will enable you to copy files saved on one disk onto a second disk without losing the originals.

3 DIR

This command will display a list of all files in the drive that the machine is "reading".

To find out more about DOS, book a place on our "How to drive a computer" course.

Task 4.7

COMBINE - AN INTEGRATED PACKAGE

This is a package that includes 3 of the most popular types of software, namely word processing, data base and spreadsheet. They can be combined to make it very simple for the user to achieve complex targets.

The 3 parts of the package are:

1) SCRIPT - the word processor,
2) FILE - the data base, and
3) PLAN - the spreadsheet.

Text can be keyed in using "Script" and saved in the normal way. Records can be entered into "File" and can then be combined with a "Script" file to produce a simple mailshot. Statistical data can be entered onto the "Plan" spreadsheet and series of figures can then be changed into a graph.

Data can be taken from a spreadsheet or graph and then inserted into a "Script" file. In this way the user can produce a printout that looks as though it has been keyed in by a trained operator.

The fact is that the package can be mastered by a complete beginner in under 2 hours!

Desk Top Publishing

What is desk top publishing? Broadly, it is a method of keying in text and graphics using a computer screen and keyboard. These are then organised to produce a printed copy. In the past this would have had to be designed using the tools of the printing trade.

In other words, it is a system which takes text files and combines them on screen with picture files into a page layout.

The final printouts have a very professional look and cost only a fraction of the price you might have to pay an artwork studio or printer.

There are many uses to which it can be put, eg:

a) NEWS-SHEETS,

b) MENUS,

c) BROCHURES.

The beauty is that it does not require any special keyboard skills. The text can be word processed by one person, the graphics designed by a second and the page organised by the desk top publisher who makes any changes needed using a "mouse" to move things around the page.

Task 4.8

Task 4.9

LEARNING TO DRIVE

Many people think that learning to drive is a simple thing to do. However, as you get older, it becomes more difficult. Some say you need one lesson for every year of your life. Just think, if you start learning at 40 and lessons cost £10 each, it could cost you £400 before you pass your test!

If you ARE thinking of learning to drive, here are some tips.

a) Take your lessons fairly early in the day as you will be fresher then and able to concentrate better.

b) Have at least 2 lessons a week to make sure you remain familiar with the car you are learning in.

c) Get plenty of practice in another car, with someone who is able to remain calm with a learner driver!

When you pass your test, remember not to go mad! After all, until then other drivers could see that you were a learner. In a way you still are but now they have no way of telling.

Country Discovery

Take your car and spend time away in delightful rural Hampshire. With peace and quiet very much in mind you can tour or stay for 2 or 3 nights in one of our inns. Each has such a warmth of atmosphere and welcome that you will feel like a valued guest from the moment you check in.

Our prices are very competitive - just look.

a) Little Inn, Liphook - £46 per person for 2 nights, £15 for each extra night.

b) The Welcome Inn, Bosham - £50 per person for 2 nights, £18 for each extra night.

c) Inn of Delight, Cadnam - £52 per person for 2 nights, £19 for each extra night.

Our prices include full English breakfast and room with bath, shower and wc. Visits to local beauty spots will be recommended by your host and in addition free maps of the area are provided.

Why not book your COUNTRY DISCOVERY break now? Take time off to relax and you will return home refreshed and rested.

Task 4.10

5 Forms for completion

Task 5.1

S T U D I O   P R I N T S   L I M I T E D

67 The Broadway   London   WC1A 4RT   Telephone: 01-957 2438

ORDER FOR COLOUR PRINTS

NAME AND ADDRESS

Miss Lucas
6 Inchcombe Street
SHEFFIELD
Yorkshire
S38 9DM

PROOF NUMBER	SIZE	NUMBER REQUIRED
2A	18 mm x 26 mm	3
6	13 mm x 18 mm	4
8B	28 mm x 36 mm	1
....	....	....
....	....	....
....	....	....

SIGNATURE ....

DATE (Date of Typing) ....

Task 5.2

S T U D I O   P R I N T S   L I M I T E D

67 The Broadway   London   WC1A 4RT   Telephone: 01-957 2438

ORDER FOR COLOUR PRINTS

NAME AND ADDRESS

Mrs Jean Andrews
75 Manning Drive
LEICESTER
LE1 6TN

PROOF NUMBER	SIZE	NUMBER REQUIRED
A/23	20 cm x 25 cm	One
A/24	30 cm x 25 cm	Two
A/16	20 cm x 25 cm	Six
....	....	....
....	....	....
....	....	....

SIGNATURE ....

DATE (Date of typing) ....

Task 5.3

TRUSTON COMPREHENSIVE SCHOOL

PUPIL'S PART-TIME EMPLOYMENT

Name of Pupil .... Keith Watson ....

Name of Employer .... Mrs Craig ....

Address .... Martins (Chemists) ....

.... 6 The Parade ....

.... TRUSTON ....

Telephone No .... 469824 ....

Business .... Chemist ....

Nature of Employment .... Stacking shelves ....

HOURS OF EMPLOYMENT

Monday		to	
Tuesday		to	
Wednesday		to	
Thursday		to	
Friday		to	
Saturday	8 am	to	12 noon
Lunch Period		to	
Total Hours		4	

Signature ....

* ~~Manager/Supervisor/~~Tutor

Date .... (Date of typing) ....

* delete as appropriate

Task 5.4

TRUSTON COMPREHENSIVE SCHOOL

PUPIL'S PART-TIME EMPLOYMENT

Name of Pupil .... Catherine Kane ....

Name of Employer .... Justifica Gowns ....

Address .... Benchford Drive ....

.... NOTTINGHAM ....

.... NG1 3SL ....

Telephone No .... 0602 735641 ....

Business .... Boutique ....

Nature of Employment .... Sales Assistant ....

HOURS OF EMPLOYMENT

Monday		to	
Tuesday		to	
Wednesday		to	
Thursday		to	
Friday		to	
Saturday	8.30am	to	5.30pm
Lunch Period		to	
Total Hours	9		

Signature ....

* ~~Manager/Supervisor~~/Tutor

Date .... (DATE OF TYPING) ....

* delete as appropriate

Task 5.5

ORDER — ORDER NO. 254

VILLIERS ENGINEERING
25 GREEN STREET
LONDON NW4 6XL

TO Praxiteles Group
8 John Adam Street
LONDON
WC2N 6EZ

DATE (DATE OF TYPING)

CODE NO.	QTY.	DESCRIPTION	UNIT PRICE £	PRICE £	PRICE p
QRS/2789	1	Oil Pressure Gauge	9.00	9	00
			TOTAL £	9	00

SIGNED

FOR EXPORT

Task 5.6

ORDER — ORDER NO. 927

VILLIERS ENGINEERING
25 GREEN STREET
LONDON NW4 6XL

TO
John Draper Plumbing Limited
28 Richard Avenue
YORK
YO1 3PA

DATE (DATE OF TYPING)

CODE NO.	QTY.	DESCRIPTION	UNIT PRICE £	PRICE £	PRICE p
Z/1562	2	Brass Taps	5.00	10	00
			TOTAL £	10	00

SIGNED

FOR EXPORT

Task 5.7

ORDER

ORDER NO. 15827

VILLIERS ENGINEERING
25 GREEN STREET
LONDON NW4 6XL

TO MS J SMITHSON
18 PARK AVENUE
BRACKNELL
BERKS
RG23 6MY

DATE
(Date of Typing)

CODE NO.	QTY.	DESCRIPTION	UNIT PRICE £	PRICE £	PRICE p
PX004	2	FILING CABINETS	95.15	190	30
			TOTAL £	190	30

SIGNED

FOR EXPORT

Task 5.8

ORDER

ORDER NO. 25/89

VILLIERS ENGINEERING
25 GREEN STREET
LONDON NW4 6XL

TO

Mr Tim Mason
6a Ludlow Gardens
ROMFORD
Essex RM6 16LP

DATE
(DATE OF TYPING)

CODE NO.	QTY.	DESCRIPTION	UNIT PRICE £	PRICE £	PRICE p
ME538	1	Lawn Mower	59.99	59	99
			TOTAL £	59	99

SIGNED

FOR EXPORT

Task 5.9

PRAXITELES
INSURANCE GROUP

PRAXITELES HOUSE · ADAM STREET · LONDON WC2N [illegible]
TELEPHONE [illegible]

To

JAMES RUSSELL ESQ
9 SPUR ROAD
BRIDGNORTH
SHROPSHIRE
WV29 6MI

Date: (Date of Typing)

Policy Number: H20095/156A

Insured: JAMES RUSSELL

Premium: £126.84

Effective Date: 1 MAY 1989

Please refer to sections 2 and 6 below.

1	[ ]	We confirm that cover has now ceased and the time on risk charge is as shown above.
2	[X]	Amendments noted. No revised document(s) necessary. Premium adjustment is as shown above.
3	[ ]	Amendments noted. Revised document(s) attached. Premium adjustment is as shown above.
4	[ ]	Duplicate document(s) attached.
5	[ ]	Policy cancelled. Return document is as shown above.
6	[X]	Please remit the premium shown above without delay.
7	[ ]	

Task 5.10

CAR PARKING PERMITS

NAME: Angela Maltby

DEPARTMENT CODE: P/5

I do/~~do not~~ drive to work. (Please delete as applicable)

REGULAR VEHICLE	Make and Model	Vauxhall Cavalier
	Registration No	D125 WAV
	Colour	Sapphire Blue
SECOND VEHICLE	Make and Model	Ford Fiesta
	Registration No	BJU 963Y
	Colour	Polar White

USUAL CAR PARK: Administration Block

I confirm that the information given above is correct, and I will inform you of any changes to these details.

SIGNED ....

DATE (Date of typing)

RSA

EXAMINATIONS BOARD

A184

TYPEWRITING SKILLS
STAGE I (ELEMENTARY)
THURSDAY 10 NOVEMBER 1988

(TIME ALLOWED - TWO HOURS)

Notes for candidates

1. Please write or type your name and centre number on each piece of your work.

2. Please assemble your completed work in the order in which it is presented in this paper and cross through any work which you do not wish to be marked.

3. Calculators, English and mother-tongue dictionaries, on-line spellcheckers and centre-prepared or manufacturers' machine manuals may be used in the examination.

You must:

1. Complete all tasks.

2. Use only the stationery provided in your answer book.

3. Insert today's date on letters, memos and forms, unless otherwise instructed.

(Penalties will be incurred if these instructions are not followed.)

TSI-1 (Autumn 1988)

-2-

TASK 1

Typist:
Please take a carbon copy on yellow paper and type an envelope

Ref EL/195

URGENT

Mr R Lovejoy
Lovejoy Enterprises Ltd
The Old Rectory
OFFORD
Cambs
CB12 4SR

Dear Richard
It was good to see you last week at the charity auction and thank you for offering the items below for sale. They will be included in our quarterly Fine Arts and Antiques Sale on December 6 1988.

Typist Inset by 6 spaces

a) Pottery lattice work ~~multi coloured~~ waste paper basket
b) Two Edwardian prints of golf courses
c) Pair of Georgian silver candlesticks circa 1790

I confirm your reserve prices, with one change, as shown on the enclosed form. As you know you did ask for a reserve of £85 for the waste paper basket. However I am glad to tell you that this piece is one of a limited edition. They are Italian made and of good quality. [I am going to show the piece illustrated in the cat.. I suggest a reserve price of £1,000 which is sufficient to attract the right amount of interest.

We hope this is acceptable and wd. like written confirmation as soon as possible in order that we can proceed with the advert..

Yours sin.
Praxiteles Group Plc

E Levine
Manager

-3-

TASK 2

Typist - please retype this article correcting the words with a circle round them.

THE ANTIQUE DEALER

Most people have an over-glamorous view about the life style of an antique dealer. The reality is often very different from the immage of the dealer at Sotheby's on the day of a picture sale. There is the fast talking auctioneer taking bids for an Old Master, the bids going up in jumps of £5,000.

However at most town and country auction rooms you will find the same people doing their circuits of regular calls. Most goods sold at local salerooms are normal household good and furniture. Occasionally a nice piece of furniture is sold but it has to be dated before 1837 to be a proper antique. The days of the easy bargain are fast disappearing

To make a living means not only visiting salerooms but also antique fairs too sell and buy. if you visit some of the London markets you will have to get up very early. Some markets start before 6.00 in the morning. Dealers may be outside all day in the winter.

-4-

Memo

TASK 3

Ref EL/421

From E Levine

Date

To Warehouse Manager

CONTAINER FOR TIMES PAST INC

I have just recd. a telephone call from Times Past about their next load. This is due out in two weeks' time ie beginning of Dec.. Please ensure that the pine ~~dressing~~ dining tables and oak gate-legged tables are not put in this shipment. Any spare space shd. be filled with mahogany side tables and satin walnut wardrobes. This shipment wl. be the last before the Christmas ~~holidays~~ break. [As you know the co. is growing ~~extremely~~ rapidly. They require a whole container of pine tables for shipment early in the new year. We need to discuss this matter in the near future. Please keep next Tuesday morning free. I will meet you in the warehouse at about 10.30 am.

-5-

TASK 4

Typist
Please type in double line spacing on A5 paper

RESERVE PRICE LIST FOR MR I GIBSON

Number	Description	Reserve Price
	Typist - leave 2 clear lines here	
27	Oak gate-legged table	£70
32	Mahogany commode	£85
60	Edwardian tray (EPNS)	£35
81	Bag of ~~hickory shafted~~ wooden golf clubs	£35
75	Two maple frames (Victorian)	£32
84	Two brass candlesticks	£30
88	Mahogany wall clock	£65
91	Wedgwood dinner service	£70
95	Palmers and Huntley biscuit tin	£15
96	Sugar shaker (EPNS)	£10

TASK 5

Typist - please use A4 paper

PRAXITELES GROUP PLC - Typist - spaced caps

Fine Art and Antiques Sale - December 6 1988

There will be a sale at the Corn Exchange building in Market Hill, Perrancastle, starting at 9.00 am. Catalogues are available thro' the agents below. Please send £2 to cover the cost of the catalogue.

VIEWING

It will be possible to view goods from 9.00-12.30 and 2.00-4.30 on the ~~preceding~~ previous day - December 5 1988. Bids may be left with the sales staff.

NOTES

Purchasers must wait until the end of the sale before paying for and collecting goods. No goods can be ~~taken~~ removed before the end of the sale.

SPECIAL INTEREST

There is an item of ~~very~~ special interest wh. is a lattice work pottery waste paper basket in bright~~y~~ colours. This is one of a limited edition. Please see catalogue for further details.

P___ G___ P___
Praxiteles House
Adam Street
LONDON
WC2N 6EZ

TASK 6

Typist - please complete the form

Name Mr R Lovejoy

Tel No 0427-379

Address Lovejoy Enterprises Ltd
The Old Rectory
OFFORD
Cambs
CB12 4SR

Stalls 2

Type of Stall Wall

Type of Stock Pictures

VAT Receipt Yes

Fees £50.00

(Page 8 of this exam paper is blank.)